Simply Rock 60s

19 Rockin' Hits of the 1960s

Arranged by Dan Coates

Simply Rock 60s is a collection of some of the greatest rock songs from one of the most pivotal decades in music history. These selections have been carefully arranged by Dan Coates for Easy Piano, making them accessible to pianists of all ages. Phrase markings, articulations, fingering, pedaling and dynamics have been included to aid with interpretation, and a large print size makes the notation easy to read.

Rock music experienced great change in the 1960s. Influenced by R & B and doo-wop of the 1950s, Ben E. King and The Drifters found success with "Save the Last Dance for Me" (1960), and Dion and the Belmonts scored a hit with "Runaround Sue" (1961). The Beatles recorded their first album *Please Please Me* in 1963, which included their hit song "Do You Want to Know a Secret?" However, as the world evolved, so did the topics of popular songs. Bob Dylan, a folk-rock pioneer, highlighted subjects ranging from war to class consciousness with his legendary "Blowin' in the Wind" (1963) and "Like a Rolling Stone" (1965). In 1964, Simon and Garfunkel responded to the assassination of President John F. Kennedy with "The Sound of Silence." The following year, The Who advocated youth rebellion with "My Generation." The British band Cream wrote of controversial topics like the psychedelic experience of a drug high ("White Room," 1968). Additionally, bands like The Impressions ("People Get Ready," 1965) and Sly & The Family Stone ("Everyday People," 1968) combined rock with elements of funk and soul. Generations of musicians and audiences have been influenced by rock music of the 1960s, forever captivated by rock's driving rhythms and clever lyrics. For these reasons and more, the hits on the following pages are exciting to explore.

After all, this is *Simply Rock 60s!*

Copyright © MMIX by ALFRED PUBLISHING CO., INC.
All rights reserved. Printed in USA.
ISBN-10: 0-7390-5878-9
ISBN-13: 978-0-7390-5878-7

Contents

Do You Want to Know a Secret?

Words and Music by
John Lennon and Paul McCartney
Arranged by Dan Coates

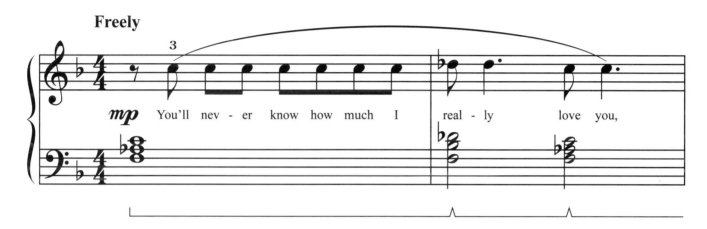

Blowin' in the Wind

Words and Music by Bob Dylan
Arranged by Dan Coates

Moderately, with a steady beat

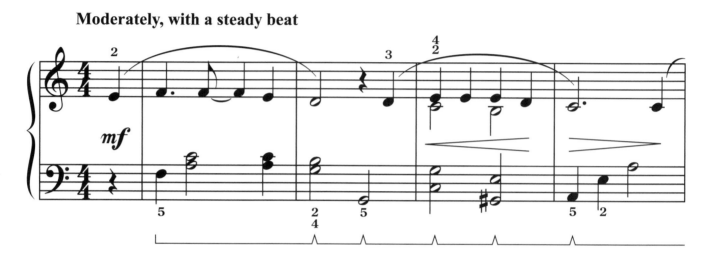

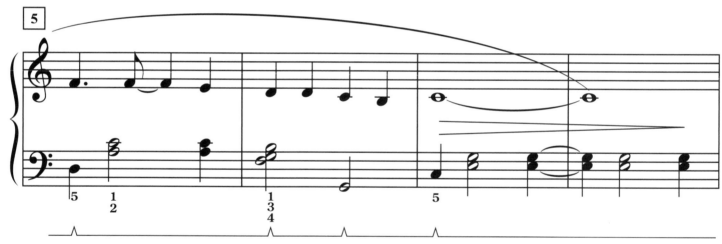

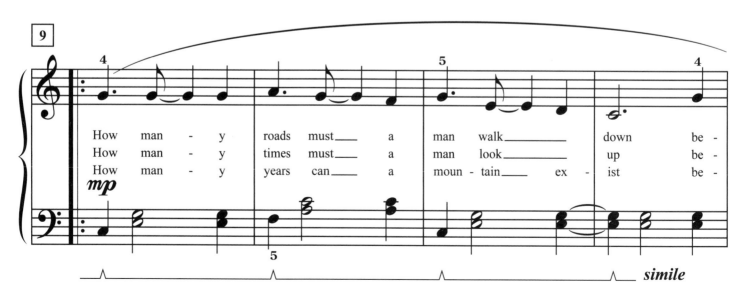

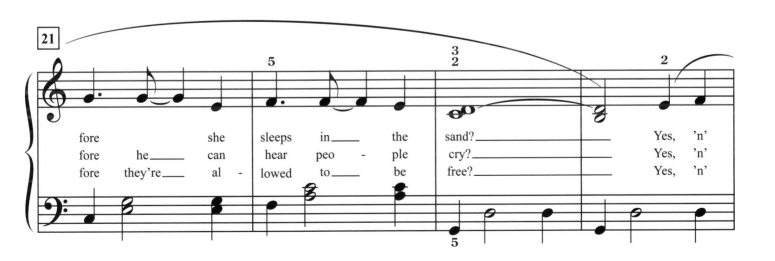

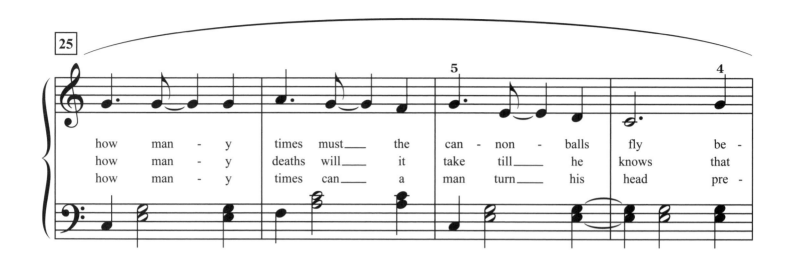

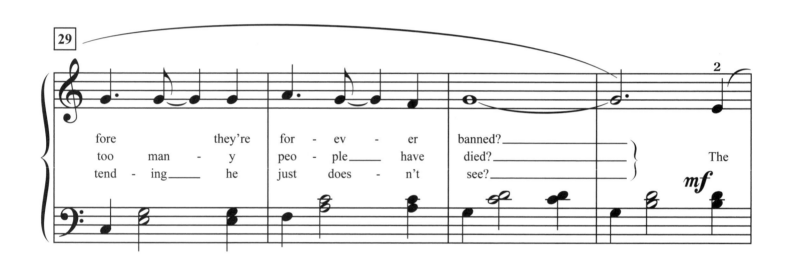

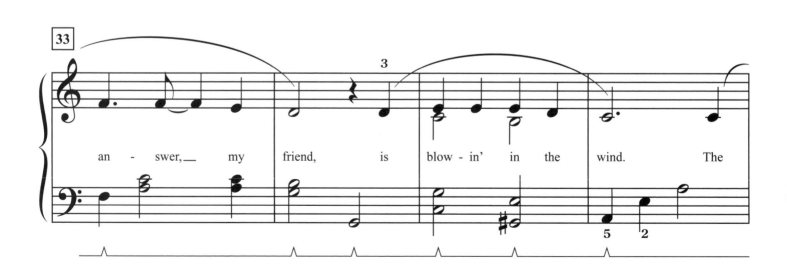

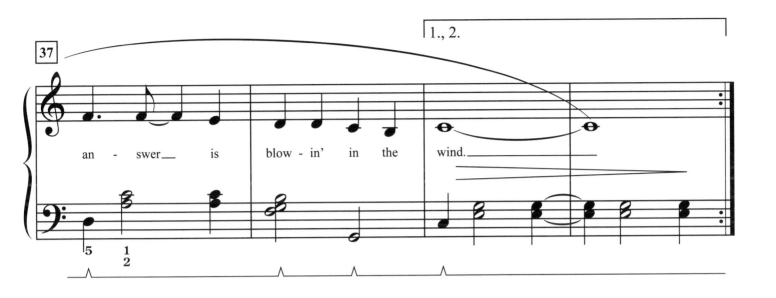

37 an - swer___ is blow - in' in the wind.___

41 3. wind. The an - swer,___ my friend, is blow - in' in the

46 wind. The an - swer___ is blow - in' in the wind.

molto rit. *p*

Gimme Some Lovin'

Words and Music by Steve Winwood,
Muff Winwood and Spencer Davis
Arranged by Dan Coates

Moderately, with a steady beat

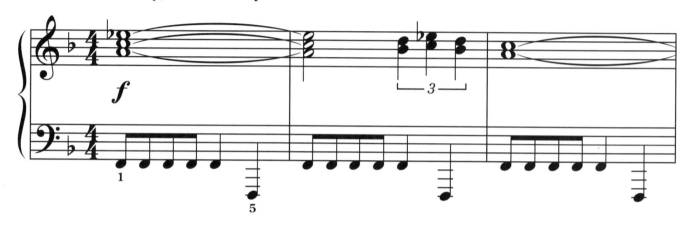

Well, my
mf

tem - p'ra - ture's ris - ing and my feet are on the floor.
feel so good;___ ev - 'ry - thing is sound - in' hot.
feel so good;___ ev - 'ry - bod - y's get - tin' high.

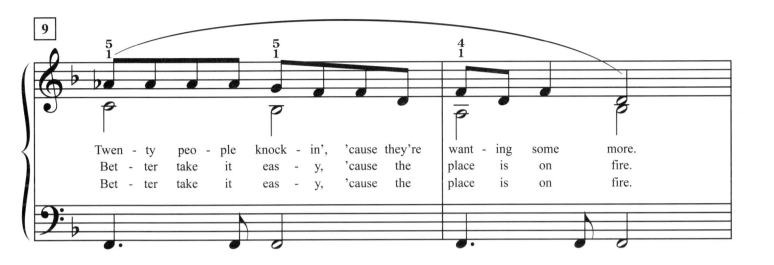

I Can See for Miles

Words and Music by Peter Townshend
Arranged by Dan Coates

Moderately fast, with a steady beat

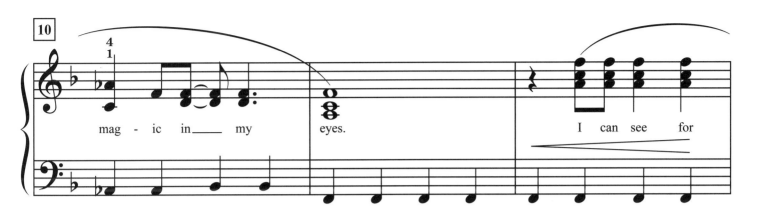

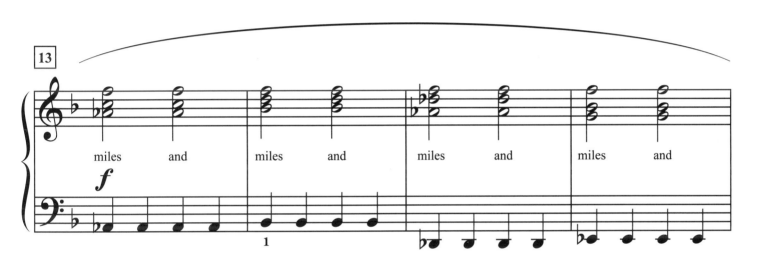

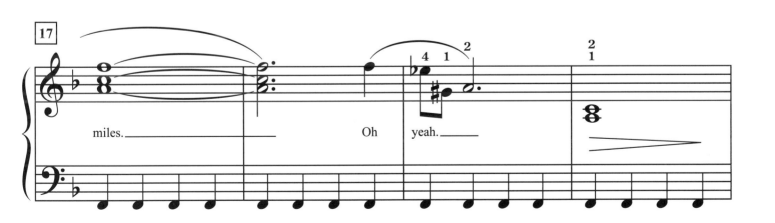

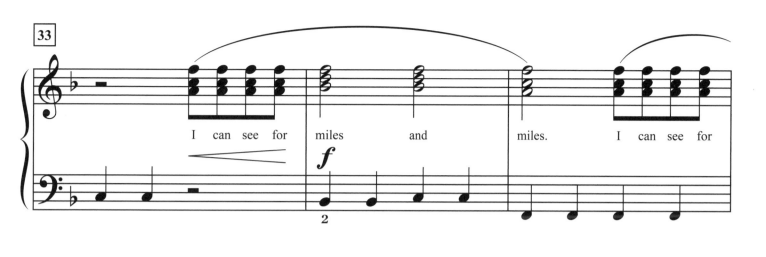

I can see for miles and miles. I can see for

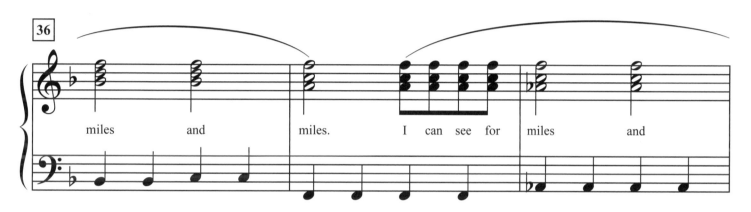

miles and miles. I can see for miles and

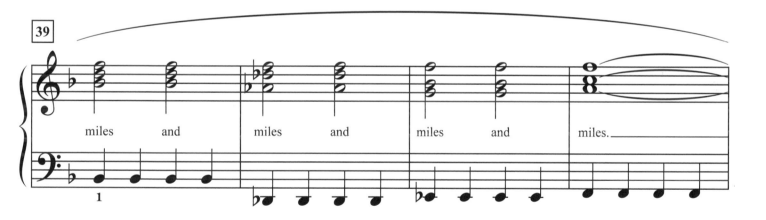

miles and miles and miles and miles.

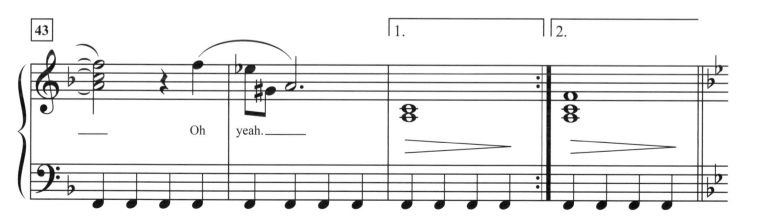

Oh yeah.

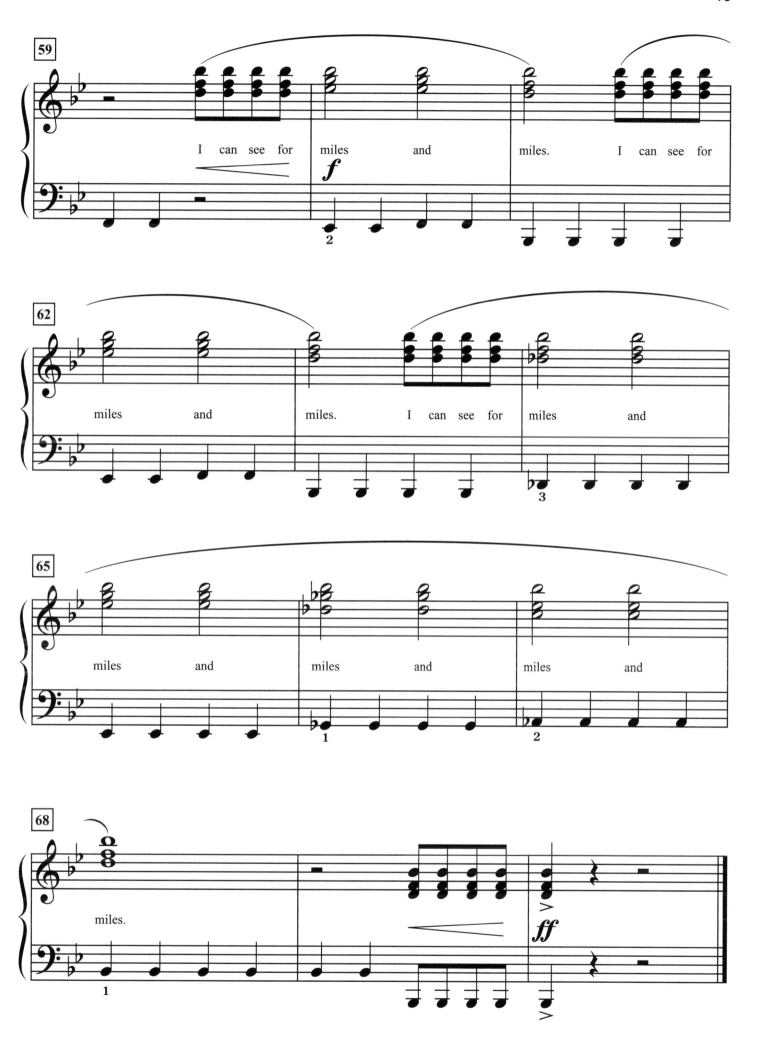

It's My Party

Words and Music by
Herb Wiener, John Gluck and Wally Gold
Arranged by Dan Coates

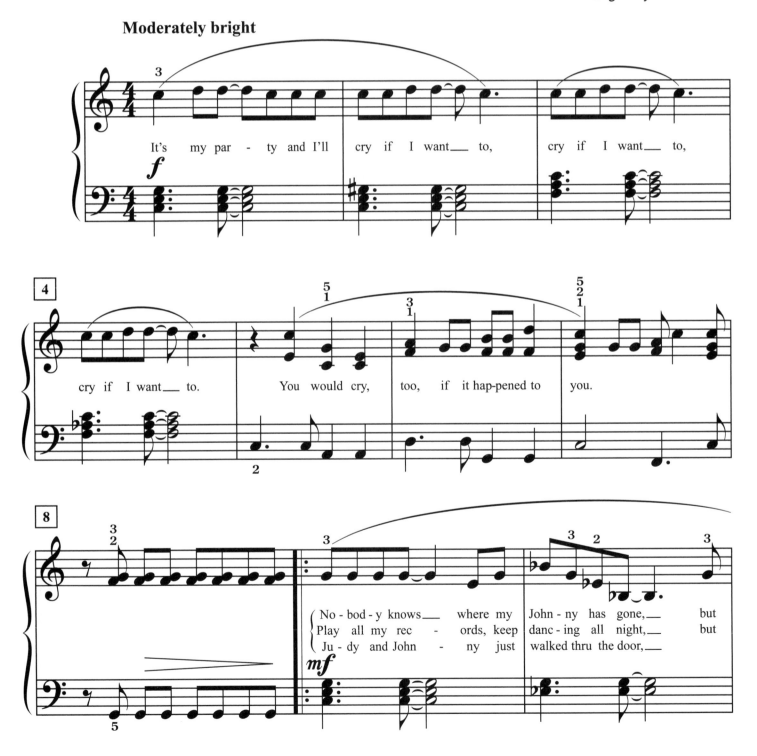

Everyday People

Words and Music by Sylvester Stewart
Arranged by Dan Coates

Moderately, with a steady beat

Some-times I'm right____ and I can be wrong.____ My own be-liefs____ are
I am no bet-ter, and neith-er are you.____ We are the same____ what-

in my song.____ The butch-er, the bank-er, the drum-mer, and then,____
ev-er we do.____ You love me, you hate me, you know me, and then,____

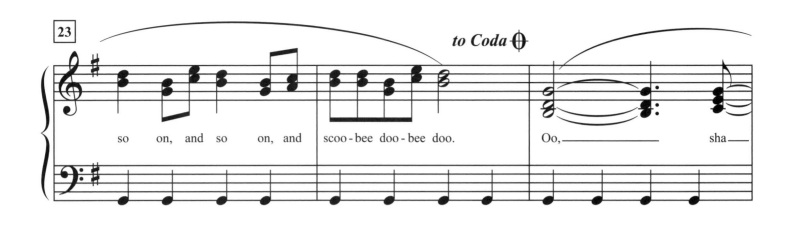

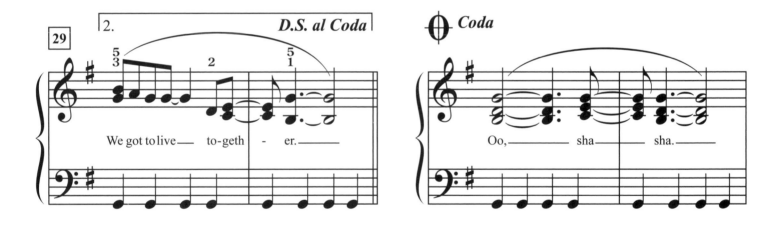

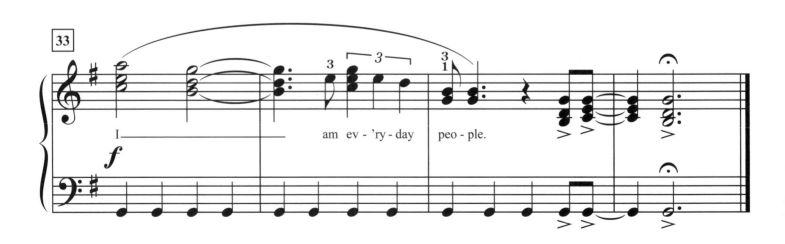

Itsy Bitsy Teenie Weenie
Yellow Polka Dot Bikini

Words and Music by
Paul J. Vance and Lee Pockriss
Arranged by Dan Coates

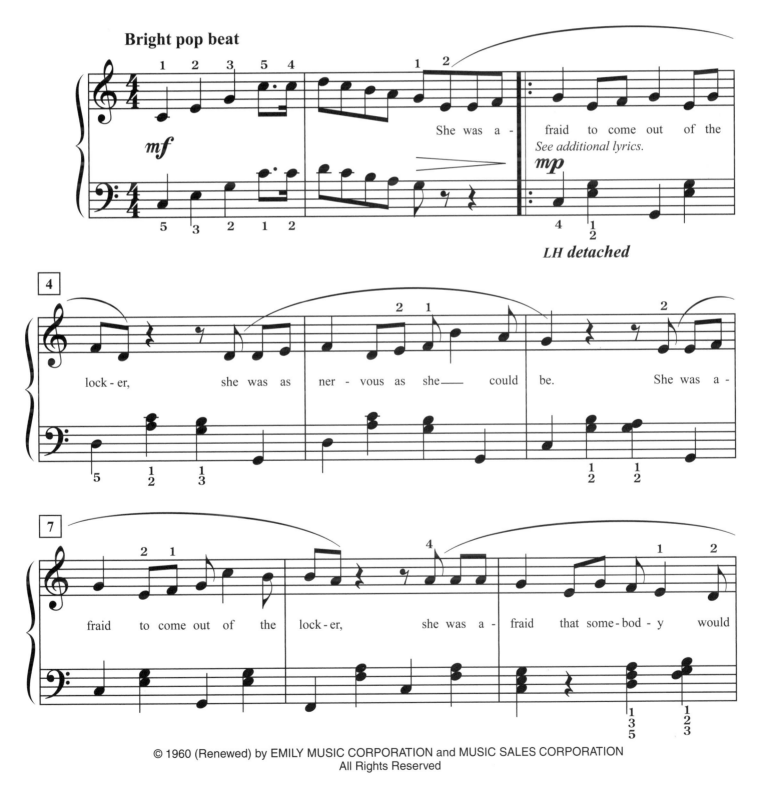

26

Verse 2:
She was afraid to come out in the open,
And so a blanket around her she wore.
She was afraid to come out in the open,
And so she sat bundled up on the shore.
(Two, three, four, tell the people what she wore.)

Verse 3:
Now she's afraid to come out of the water,
And I wonder what she's gonna do.
Now she's afraid to come out of the water,
And the poor little girl's turning blue.
(Two, three, four, tell the people what she wore.)

Johnny Angel

Words by Lyn Duddy
Music by Lee Pockriss
Arranged by Dan Coates

Moderately slow

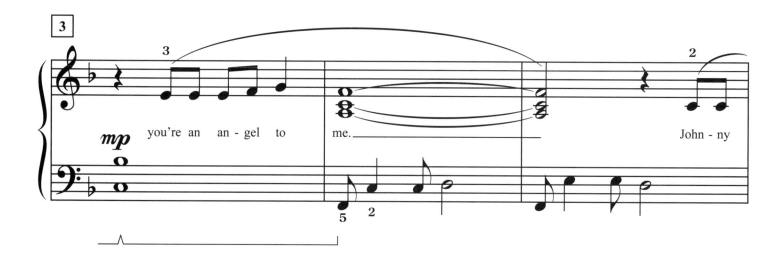

sist. But he does-n't ev - en know that I_____ ex -

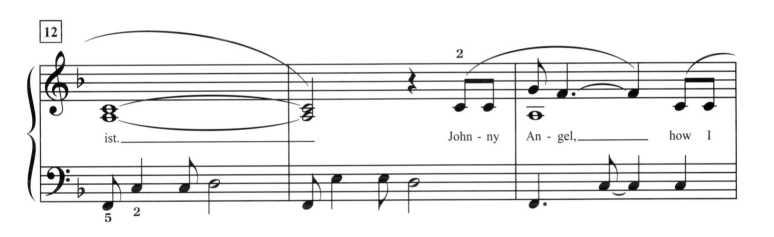

ist._____ John - ny An - gel,_____ how I

want him,_____ how I tin - gle when he pass - es by. Ev - 'ry

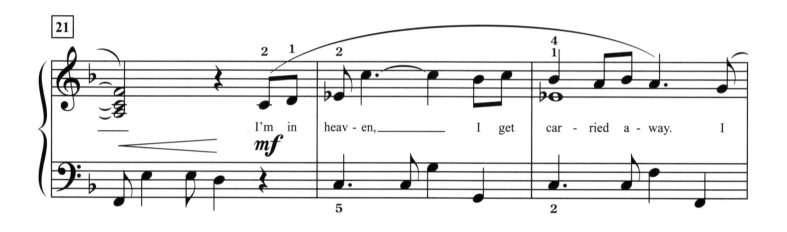

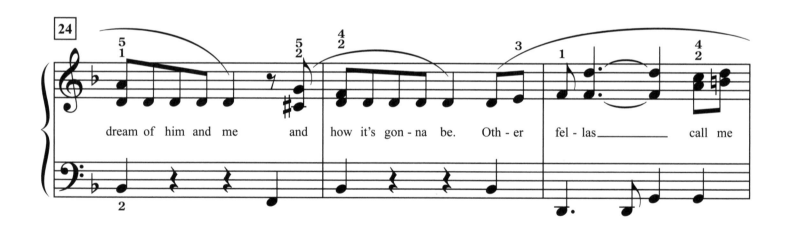

An - gel,_____ 'cause I love him,_____ and I pray that some - day he'll love

mp

me. And to - geth - er we will see how love - ly heav - en can

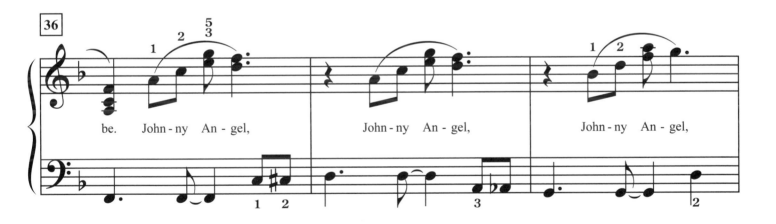

be. John - ny An - gel, John - ny An - gel, John - ny An - gel,

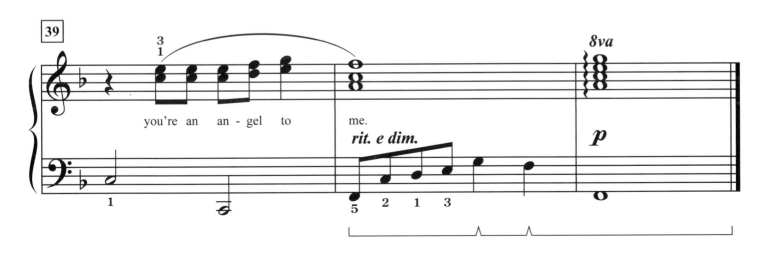

you're an an - gel to me.

rit. e dim.

8va

p

My Generation

Words and Music by Peter Townshend
Arranged by Dan Coates

34

The Night They Drove Old Dixie Down

Words and Music by Robbie Robertson
Arranged by Dan Coates

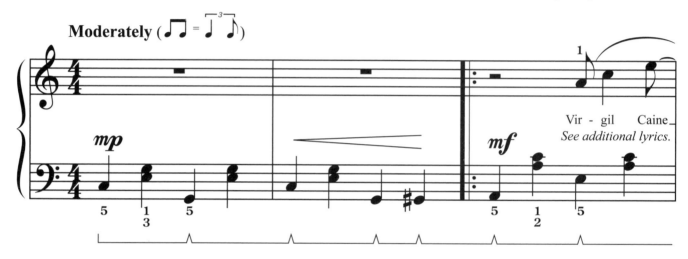

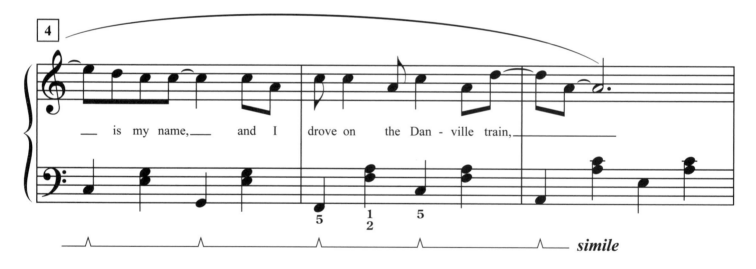

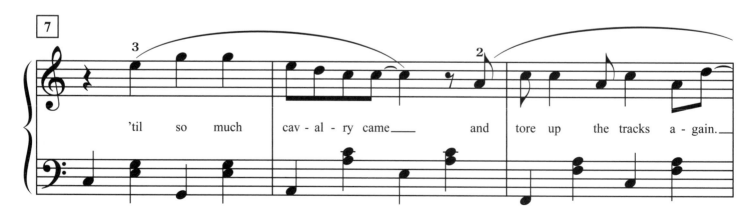

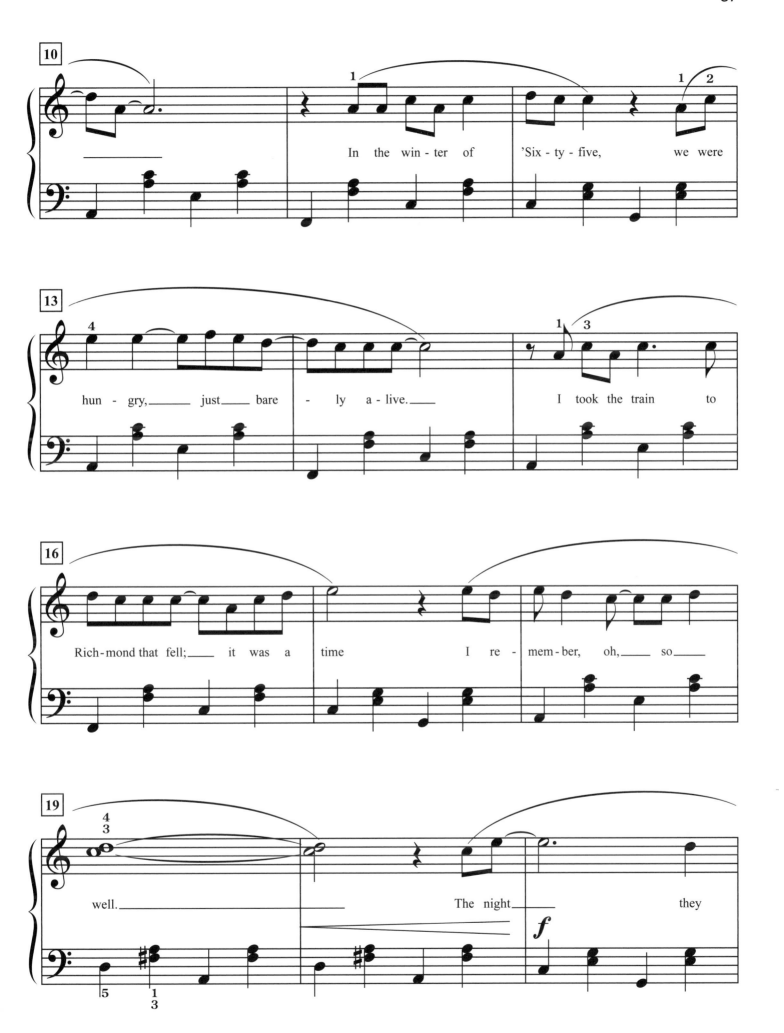

drove old Dix - ie down.___ And all the bells were ring - in' the

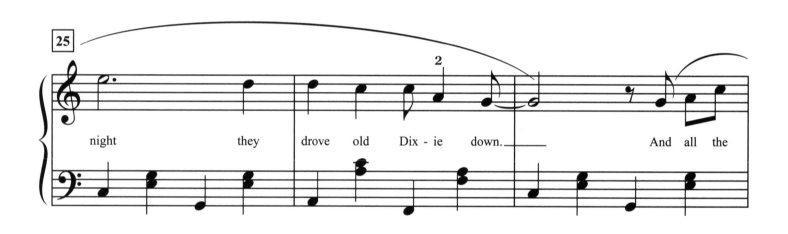

night they drove old Dix - ie down.___ And all the

peo - ple were sing - in'. They went, "La la la la la la,___

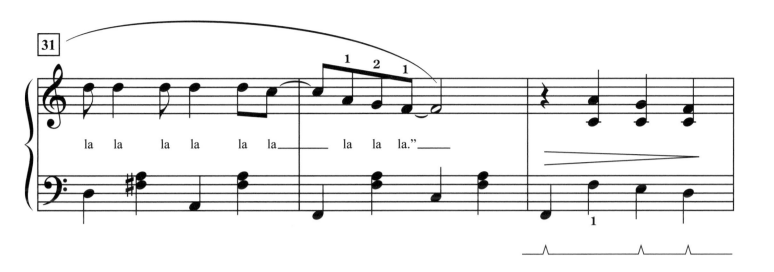

la la la la la la la la la."

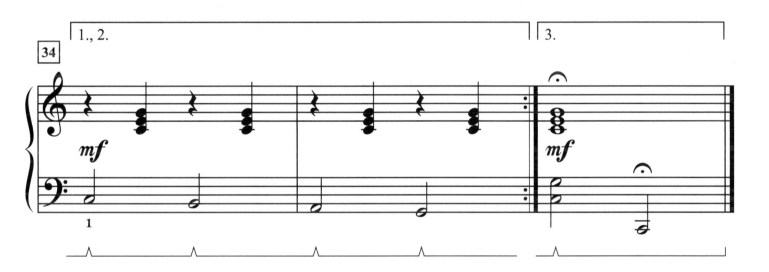

Verse 2:
Back with my wife in Tennessee,
And one day she said to me,
"Virgil, quick come see.
There goes the Robert E. Lee."
Now, I don't mind I'm choppin' wood,
And I don't care if my money's no good.
Just take what you need and leave the rest,
But they should never have taken the very best.

Verse 3:
Like my father before me,
I'm a working man.
And like my brother before me,
I took a rebel stand.
Well, he was just eighteen, proud and brave,
But a Yankee laid him in his grave.
I swear by the blood below my feet,
You can't raise the Caine back up
When it's in defeat.

Mr. Tambourine Man

Words and Music by Bob Dylan
Arranged by Dan Coates

Moderately, with a steady beat

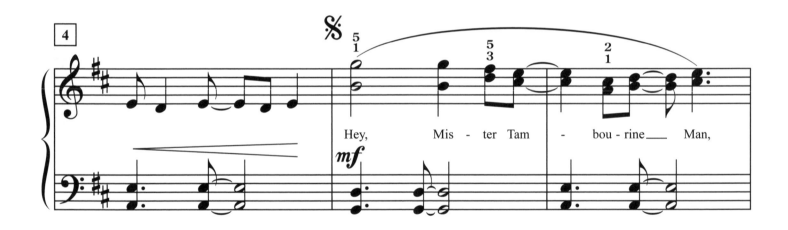

Hey, Mis - ter Tam - bou - rine___ Man,

play a song___ for me.___ I'm not sleep - y and there

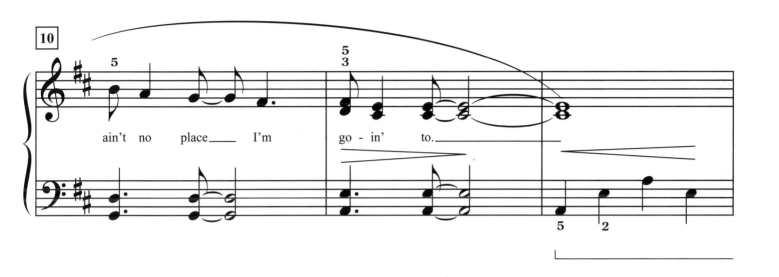

ain't no place___ I'm go - in' to.___

𝆑 Hey, Mis - ter Tam - bou - rine___ Man, play a song___ for me.___

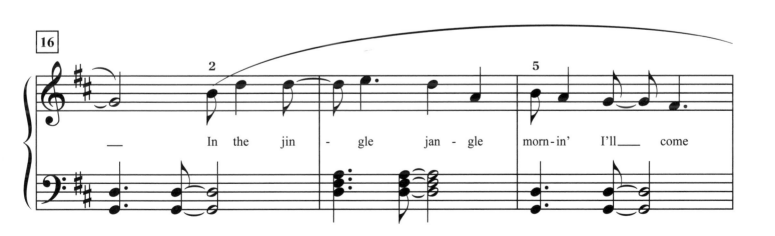

___ In the jin - gle jan - gle morn - in' I'll___ come

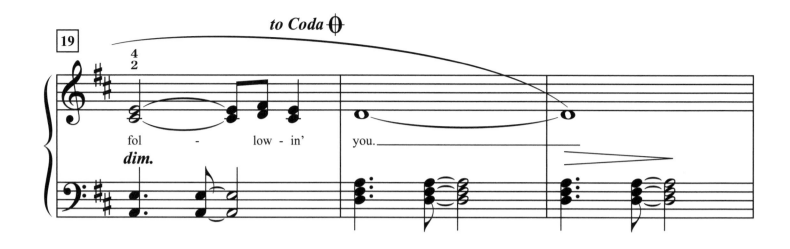

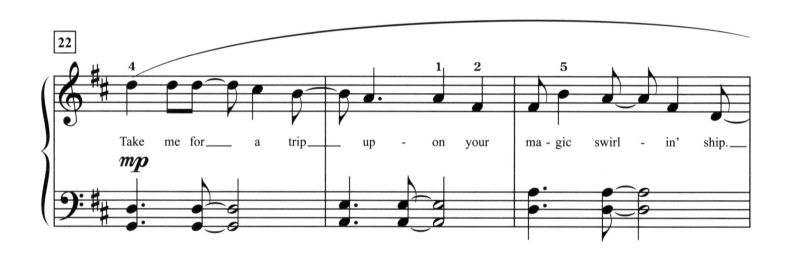

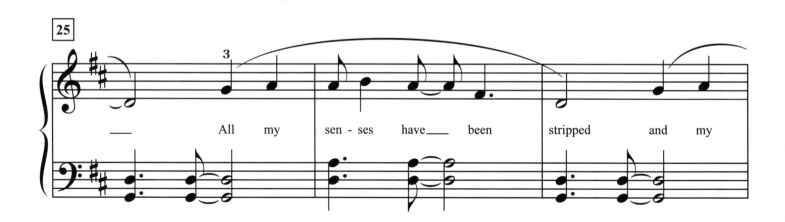

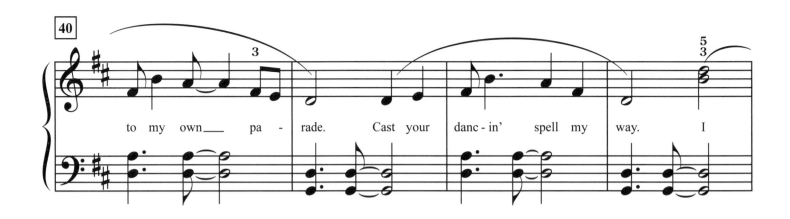

to my own___ pa - rade. Cast your danc - in' spell my way. I

D.S. al Coda

pro - mise to go un - der it.___

Coda

you.

mp

rit.

p

Ode to Billie Joe

Words and Music by Bobbie Gentry
Arranged by Dan Coates

Verse 2:
Papa said to Mama, as he passed around the black-eyed peas,
"Well, Billie Joe never had a lick o' sense. Pass the biscuits, please."
And Mama said it was a shame about Billie Joe anyhow.
"Seems like nothin' ever comes to no good up on Choctaw Ridge.
And now Billie Joe McAllister's jumped off the Tallahatchie Bridge."

Verse 3:
Brother said he recollected when he and Tom and Billie Joe
Put a frog down my back at the Carroll County picture show.
And wasn't I talkin' to him after church last Sunday night?
"I'll have another piece of apple pie, you know, it don't seem right.
I saw him at the sawmill yesterday on Choctaw Ridge,
And now you tell me Billie Joe's jumped off the Tallahatchie Bridge."

Verse 4:
Mama said, "Child, what's happened to your appetite?
I've been cookin' all mornin' and you haven't touched a single bite.
That nice young preacher, Brother Taylor, dropped by today.
Said he'd be pleased to have dinner on Sunday. Oh, by the way,
He said he saw a girl that looked a lot like you up on Choctaw Ridge.
And she an' Billie Joe was throwin' somethin' off the Tallahatchie Bridge."

Verse 5:
A year has come and gone since we heard the news 'bout Billie Joe.
Brother married Becky Thompson. They bought a store in Tupelo.
There was a virus goin' 'round. Papa caught it and he died last spring.
And now Mama doesn't seem to want to do much of anything.
And me I spend a lot of time pickin' flowers up on Choctaw Ridge.
And drop them into the muddy water off the Tallahatchie Bridge.

People Get Ready

Words and Music by Curtis Mayfield
Arranged by Dan Coates

Moderate rhythm and blues

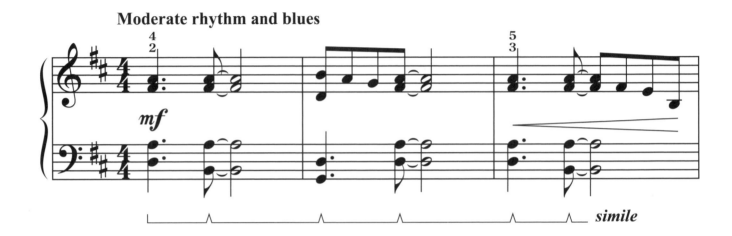

Peo - ple, get read - y, there's a train a - com - in'. You
Peo - ple, get read - y, for the train to Jor - dan,

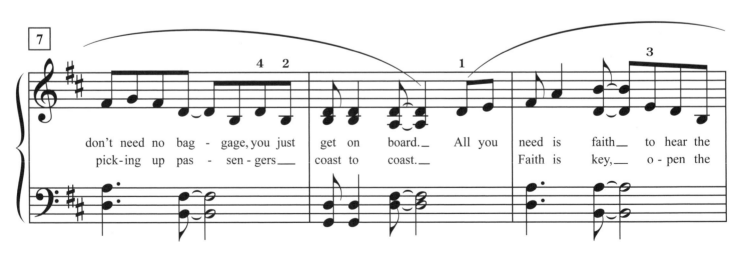

don't need no bag - gage, you just get on board.__ All you need is faith__ to hear the
pick - ing up pas - sen - gers__ coast to coast.__ Faith is key,__ o - pen the

die - sel hum - min'.
doors and board__ 'em.

Don't need no tick - et, you just
There's hope for all__ a - mong those

thank the Lord.__
loved the most.__

to Coda

1.

2.

There ain't no room_____ for the hope - less sin - ner who would hurt all man - kind just to

save__ his own.__ Have pit - y on those__ whose chanc - es grow thin - ner, for there's

no hid - ing place____ a - gainst the king - dom's throne.____

D.S. al Coda

Save the Last Dance for Me

Words by Doc Pomus
Music by Mort Shuman
Arranged by Dan Coates

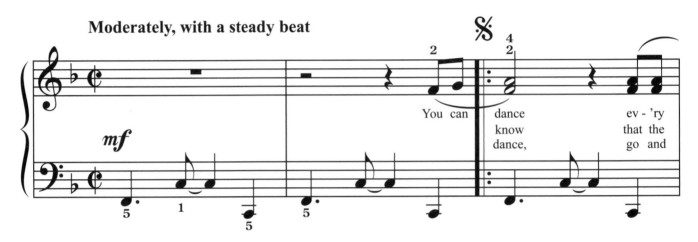

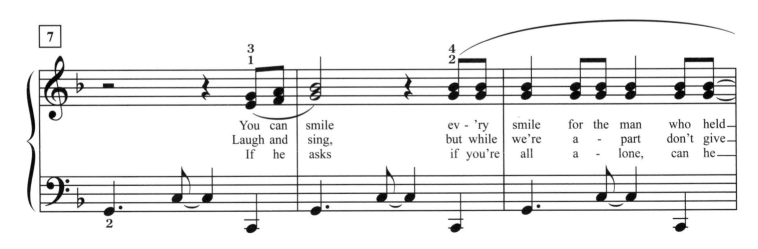

your hand 'neath the pale moon - light.
your heart to an - y - one.
take you home, you must tell him no.
But don't for -

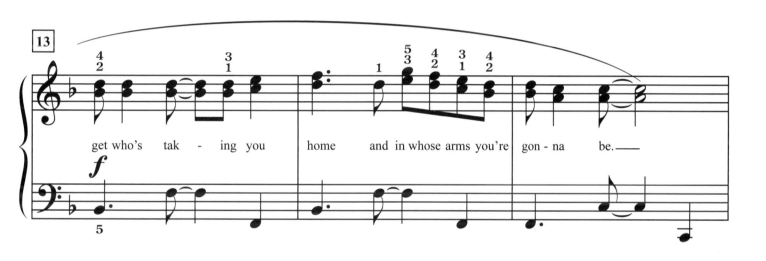

get who's tak - ing you home and in whose arms you're gon - na be.

to Coda

So dar - lin', save the last dance for

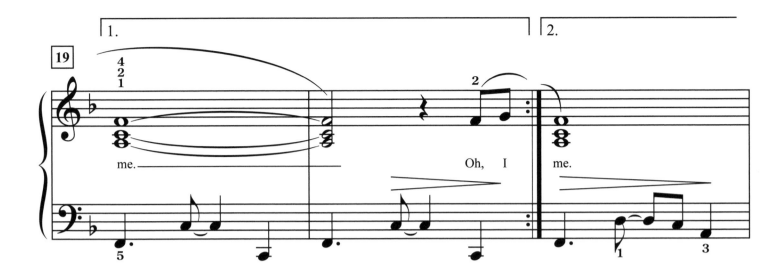

D.S. al Coda

I love you, oh, so much.

You can

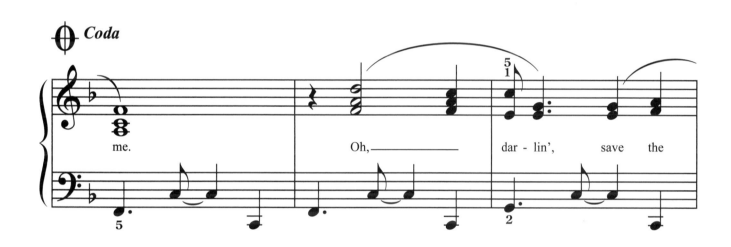

Coda

me.

Oh,⎯⎯ dar - lin', save the

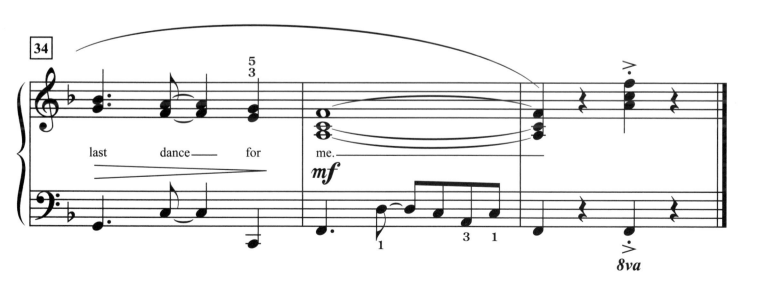

last dance⎯ for me.

mf

8va

The Sound of Silence

Words and Music by Paul Simon
Arranged by Dan Coates

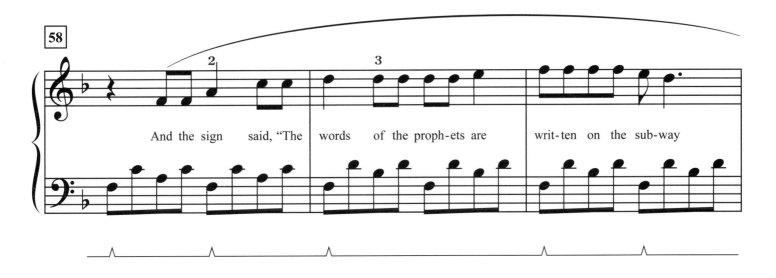

And the sign said, "The words of the proph-ets are writ-ten on the sub-way

walls and tene-ment halls" and whis-pered_____ in the

dim.

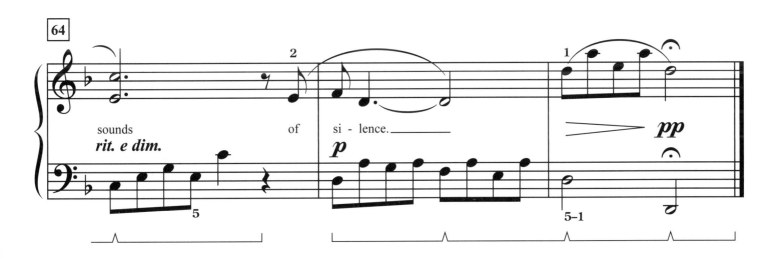

sounds of si - lence._____

rit. e dim.

Sunshine of Your Love

Words and Music by Jack Bruce,
Pete Brown and Eric Clapton
Arranged by Dan Coates

Moderately, with a rock beat

It's get-ting near dawn,—
I'm with you, my love,—
when the

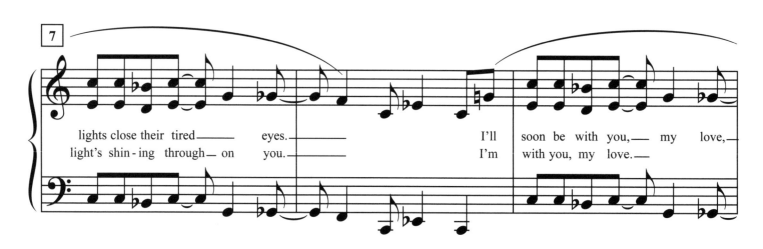

lights close their tired—— eyes.——
light's shin-ing through— on you.——
I'll soon be with you,— my love,—
I'm with you, my love.—

to give you my dawn ___ sur - prise. ___   I'll
It's the morn - ing and just ___ we two. ___   I'll

be with you, dar - ling, soon. ___   I'll be with you when ___ the stars ___
stay with you, dar - ling, now. ___   I'll stay with you till ___ my seas ___

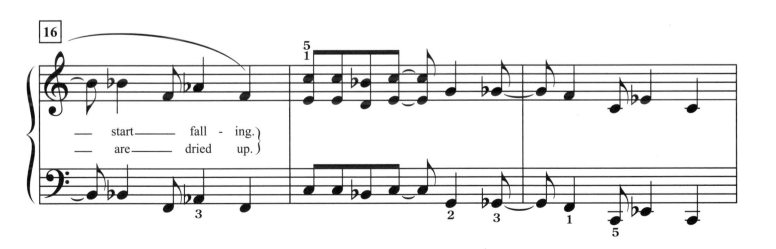

___ start ___ fall - ing.
___ are ___ dried up.

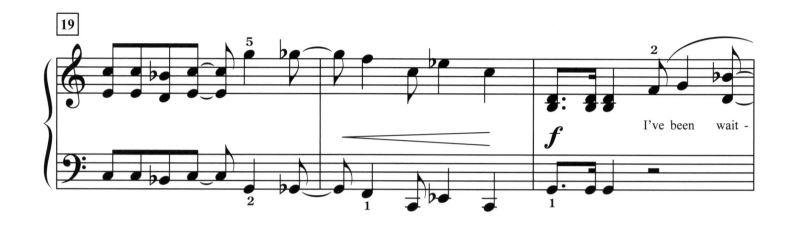

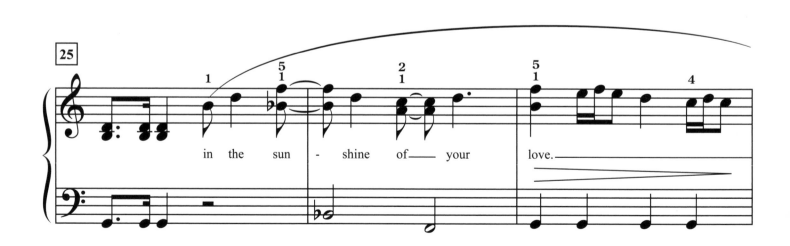

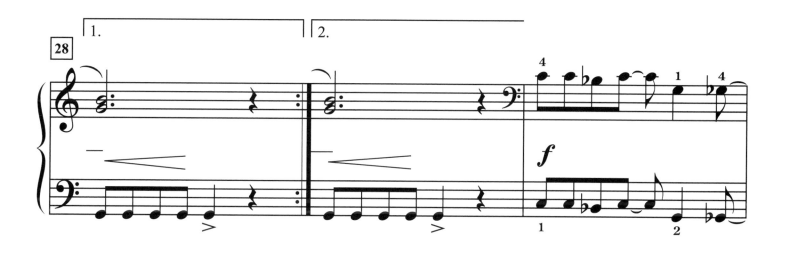

Runaround Sue

Words and Music by
Dion DiMucci and Ernest Maresca
Arranged by Dan Coates

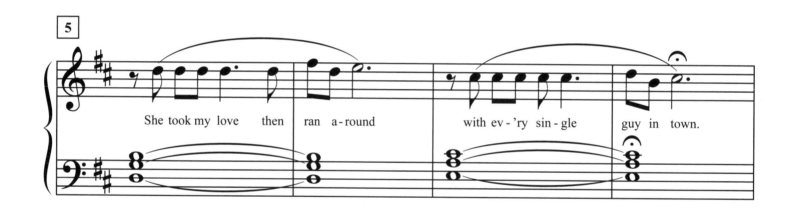

hayp,   hayp,   bum - da ha - dy, ha - dy,   hayp!

I should have known it from the   ver - y   start,___   this girl will leave you with a
I miss her lips   and the   smile on her face,___   the touch of her hair and this

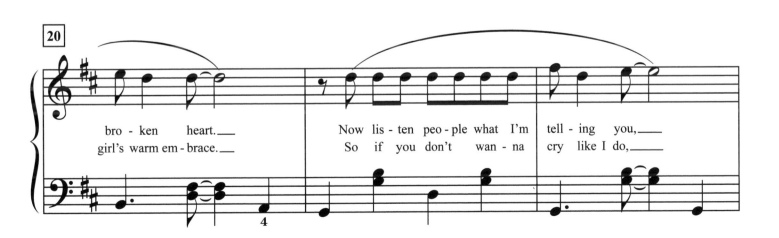

bro - ken   heart.___   Now lis - ten peo - ple what I'm   tell - ing   you,___
girl's warm em - brace.___   So   if you don't   wan - na   cry like I do,___

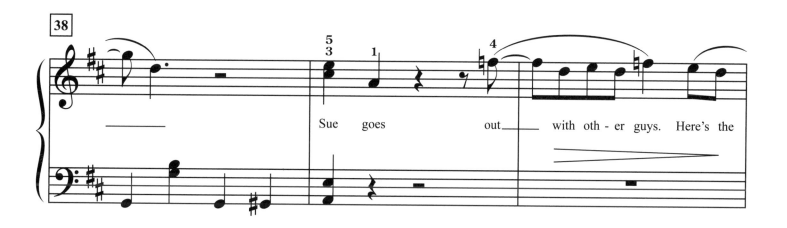

Sue goes out__ with oth - er guys. Here's the

mor - al of the sto - ry from the guy who knows,__ I fell in love and my love

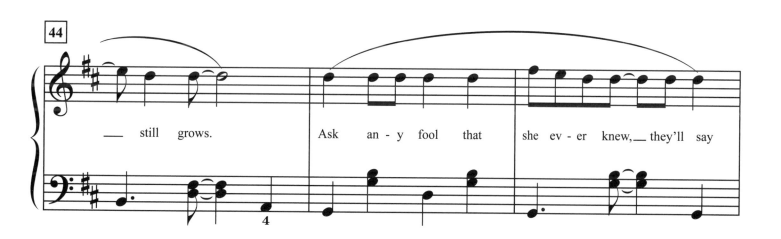

__ still grows. Ask an - y fool that she ev - er knew,__ they'll say

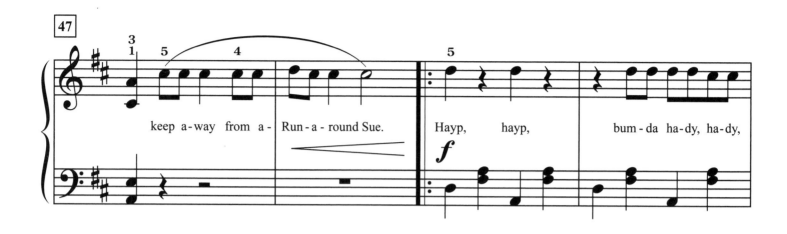

keep a-way from a- Run-a-round Sue. Hayp, hayp, bum-da ha-dy, ha-dy,

hayp, hayp, bum-da ha-dy, ha-dy, hayp, hayp, bum-da ha-dy, ha-dy,

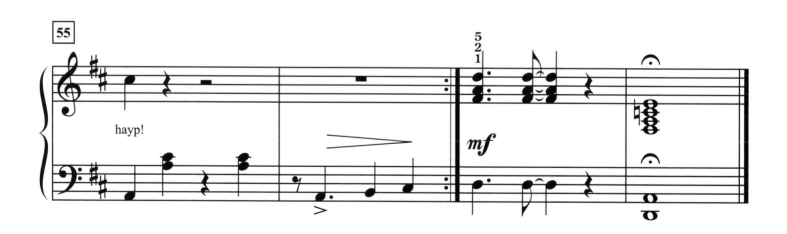

hayp!

White Room

Words and Music by
Jack Bruce and Pete Brown
Arranged by Dan Coates

Moderately, with a rock beat

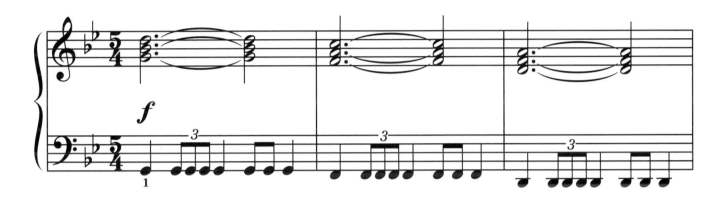

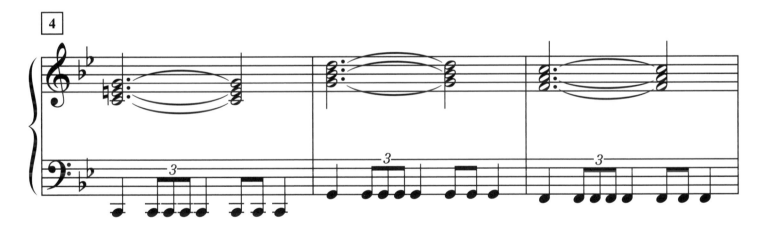

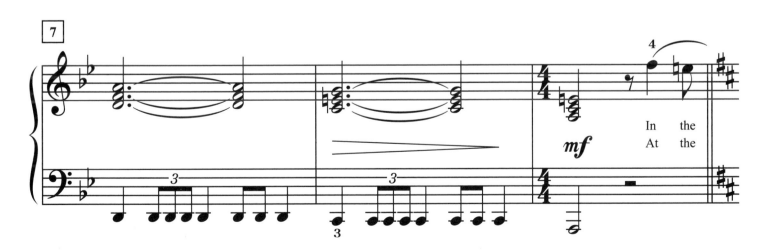

In the
At the

white room with black cur - tains near the sta - tion.
no strings could se - cure you at the sta - tion.
par - ty she was kind - ness in the hard crowd.

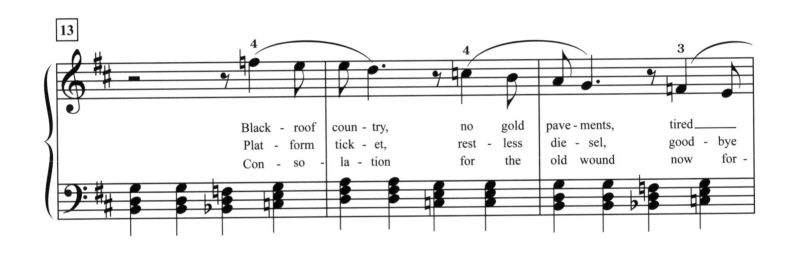

Black - roof coun - try, no gold pave - ments, tired_____
Plat - form tick - et, rest - less die - sel, good - bye
Con - so - la - tion for the old wound now for -

star - lings.
win - dows. Sil - ver hors - es ran down
got - ten. I walked in - to such a
Yel - low ti - gers crouched in

moon - beams ... in ... your ... dark ... eyes. ... Dawn ... light
sad ... time ... at ... the ... sta - ... tion. ... As ... I
jun - gles ... in ... her ... dark ... eyes. ... She's ... just

smiles_____ ... on ... you ... leav - ... ing ... my ... con - ... tent - ... ment.
walked_ ... out, ... felt ... my ... own_ ... need ... just ... be - ... gin - ... ning.
dress - ... ing ... good - ... bye ... win - ... dows, ... tired_____ ... star - ... lings.

I'll ... wait_____ ... in ... this ... place_____ ... where ... the
I'll ... wait_____ ... in ... the ... queue_____ ... when ... the
I'll ... sleep_____ ... in ... this ... place_____ ... with ... the

mp

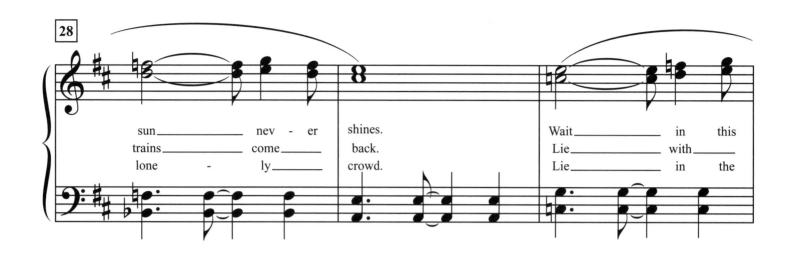

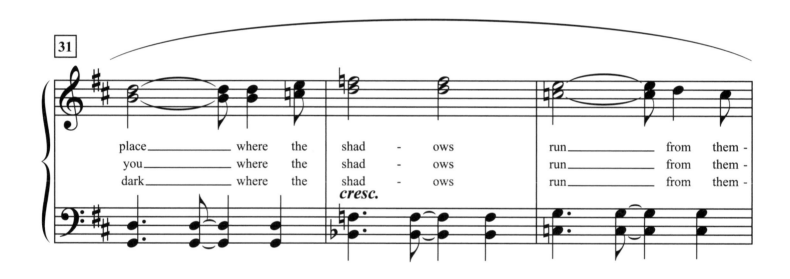

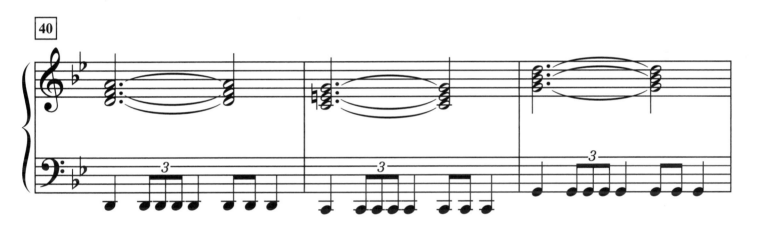

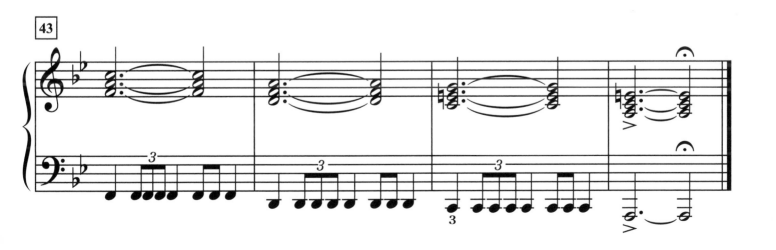

A Whiter Shade of Pale

Words and Music by
Keith Reid and Gary Brooker
Arranged by Dan Coates

Moderately slow

ghost - ly,   turned a   whit - er____   shade of   pale.____

pale.____   mp

cresc.   And so it

was _____ that lat - er, as the mill - er told his

tale, _____ that her face, at first just ghost - ly, turned a

whit - er _____ shade of pale. _____

rit. e dim.